THE FUTURE IS HERE

—A MURDER MYSTERY—

Fifth Book in the Zuma Mystery Series

JEROME RABOW, PH.D.

ISBN 978-1-955156-70-7 (paperback)
ISBN 978-1-955156-71-4 (digital)

Copyright © 2021 by Jerome Rabow, Ph.D.

All rights reserved. No part of this publication may be reproduced, distributed, or transmitted in any form or by any means, including photocopying, recording, or other electronic or mechanical methods without the prior written permission of the publisher. For permission requests, solicit the publisher via the address below.

Rushmore Press LLC
1 800 460 9188
www.rushmorepress.com

Printed in the United States of America

TABLE OF CONTENTS

1 5
2 11
3 14
4 18
5 22
6 24
7 27
8 33
9 35
10 39
11 42
12 46
13 49
14 52
15 55
16 58
17 62
18 66
19 70
20 73
21 76

1

Sitting at the head of a table in a large board room was a square-shouldered man in his fifties. There were six more executive types sitting around, sipping coffee or water; all their attention was directed toward the head of the table.

The man said, "We need Black people. If we don't get them, we're gonna lose one goddamn big contract. Who can get some damn Blacks in my company?"

Jack, one of the seated males, responded. "What type of jobs? What skills do we need?"

He replied, "I don't care. Just get them; we need them. Someone with a good college education and the right race is what we need. This is rushed. Do you all understand the importance of this? You need to get back to me by the end of the day. Are we clear?"

He gave the room one last look before deciding that he's done for the day.

"Jack, let's go grab a bite and let them do their work."

Jerry Fleishman, the headman, and Jack then left.

On the way down the hall, they saw a Black male.

They approached him, and Jerry asked, "Are you looking for a job?"

"Sure," the Black man responded, albeit surprised. "If it pays better than the one I have."

"What do you do?"

"I work for you in this company. I'm a security guard."

"Oh, well . . . we had something else in mind."

"I learn very quickly. I'm smart and I am going to—"

Before the man could finish, Jerry had already begun to walk away with Jack following him.

They entered a deli on the third street mall in Santa Monica. It was pretty crowded. Jack and the headman joined the long queue, and after a while, they were finally next. The man behind the counter greeted them.

"Nice to see you gentlemen again. I just baked this great new bread." He slices three pieces and pours syrup on top.

"Neither of us eat bread. Thank you."

"Take it anyway; I already cut it."

"Could you please cut me three pieces of that roast beef and trim the fat? Put some coleslaw and a couple of pickles, and some potato salad. That should do it for me."

Jack added, "Do the same for me—but with pastrami instead of the roast beef and some extra mustard."

"You got it."

They waited for their plates, and when their orders arrived, they took their seats.

"I'm going to make some calls when we get back," Jack said. "I know a number of programs and deans at Ivy League schools, but I'll start with Harvard and MIT."

"Why are you going there? That's way too far a reach. It would be expensive to relocate anyone from there. In this city we have really good schools like UCLA, USC, and Caltech. Besides, Caltech has a great artificial intelligence program. I know they have lots of Indians."

"Jerry, I didn't know you wanted an Indian. I thought you said you wanted to hire a Black person. I don't know if Caltech has any Black people in their artificial intelligence program."

"Try, Jack. And what about Berkeley? They also have a fine program in tech…"

Jack considered this before responding, "Would you accept a marketing person? I have a great contact at USC."

Jerry replied, "I don't know. We need someone who is Black. I think it's better if they have STEM training. But you make your call to USC. Maybe we'll hire two Black people. That will really make us look good to the community and to all future contractors who want to hire us."

Jack nodded. "I'll make the calls right when we get back."

It took Jack half an hour before he managed to reach the head of a department at Caltech. He carefully described what his company needs.

"It just so happens that I have the kind of person you are looking for right now sitting in my office," said the department head.

"Great. Can you give me his cell number now? I'll get the president of our company, Jerry Fleishman, to call him. What's his name?" Jack shifted the phone in his hand as he took a pen and piece of paper with the other. "Jerome Blackwell? Thank you. I'm writing his number down."

"Jerry, I think I found someone who might be more than just a face for the company. He's a grad student finishing up at Caltech, and the chair was laudatory about him. His name is Jerome Blackwell, and I said you would call him. Here's his number."

Jerry was pleased and jumped on the phone call.

"Hi, Mr. Blackwell. Let me introduce myself. My name is Jerry Fleishman, and I'm the president of Stillwell Corporation."

Jerome Blackwell thanked him and said something that pleased Jerry even more.

"Oh, you know about us and what we do. Well, that makes it easier. I'm interested in offering you a job in our artificial intelligence dept. We have about five people working there now."

Jerry couldn't help but grin, delighted by the smooth flow of the conversation.

"You know the people? That's amazing. Would you be interested in joining us?"

He paused as he listened to Jerome's response. "I like that you don't beat around the bush . . . Yes, I think we can offer you two hundred thousand dollars a year . . . You want to bring in some others from your school? How many more people will you need to work with you?"

Jerry considered Jerome's response for a bit, doing the math in his head. "Four more plus you—that makes five. And you say you want the same salary for the five of you—that's a million there. And you will need a new lab because you know that our lab is not up-to-date for the kind of work you will be doing . . . It's nothing personal, but the kind of work I plan to do with my team for your company requires the latest in laboratory science and safety and security. . . Let me go over this with you, Mr. Blackwell. It's going to cost me three to five million, depending on the type of building. Possibly even more than that because you say it has to be soundproof and dustproof—and not subject to movement or swaying from the building. Okay, that's a total of six million."

Jerome talked some more, and Jack could see that Jerry was growing a bit less patient as the talk went on. "I'm ready. When can you start? We'd like you right away . . . You're not finished yet? So . . . You want all inventions and patents to be given to the five of you equally? That's a lot to ask for, Mr. Blackwell. You're only twenty-six years old. Mr. Blackwell, I didn't make two hundred thousand dollars a year 'til I was forty."

Jack could only hear one side of the conversation, but he could guess how it was going based on Jerry's shift in mood. Jerry frowned at him and put the phone on loudspeaker just in time for Jack to hear Jerome say, "By the time I'm forty, Mr. Fleishman, I will be earning at least a million a year. It may be a lot, but you need me more than I need you."

Jerry rolled his eyes. "Why is that?"

"One reason is that I know you don't have Black people in your company, and I fit the bill. Not only do I fit the bill, but my team also fits the bill. We become the new and modern face to Stillwell Corporation. I have two women on my team—one white and the other Black. I have a Latino and an Indian male. But the biggest reason is that we are going to invent things that you can't imagine. We are the future. And we will make you and your company rich and famous."

Jerry discussed a few more things with Jerome before the call ended. He tossed the phone back to Jack, who noticed that the glint of excitement had returned to Jerry's face.

"Jack, I'm really impressed with the sense of confidence expressed by this young man you found. Good job."

That afternoon, Jerry Fleishman released a press release and made a public announcement inviting all the media outlets in Santa Monica to a ceremony in two days. He had never done anything like this before, and he was genuinely excited and proud. He told Jack, who was then surprised because Jerry rarely expressed such feelings.

And the day of the ceremony came.

"Ladies and gentlemen, we are proud to introduce to you the new members of the Stillwell Corporation. We have been in the business of staying ahead of our competition, and the recent recruitment of these five brilliant students from Caltech will allow us to continue to be at the forefront of inventing items that make the lives of all

Americans safer and easier. The citizens of Santa Monica will be able to take pride that the Stillwell Corporation—located right here—is doing good things for the world as well as providing preference for employment opportunities to all citizens of Santa Monica.

It is my pleasure to introduce—standing next to me and going from right to left—Sara Winter, Vicki Cummings, Joseph Castro, Ramesh Kumar, and Jerome Blackwell. They have asked me to prevent questions being asked about what they are working on. But they have also said they would be happy to make an announcement when they have completed their first invention for the Stillwell Corporation.

We are proud and lucky to land such a talented group. We know that you will make their working, and possibly living, in Santa Monica as pleasant and neighborly as you can.

Thank you for your attendance in this important event in the Stillwell Corporation's efforts to be on the cutting edge of the application of knowledge to the issues of daily living."

2

Detective Joe Zuma had a nice quiet dinner with Claudia, his wife of seven years in his very happy second marriage, at their favorite restaurant in Santa Monica—the Shangri-La. They were getting ready for bed at around eleven o'clock when Zuma saw a message from Pat Vasquez, his close colleague and fellow detective. Pat called, and he immediately picked it up.

"Joe, I'm sorry to bother you so late, but I thought you might have wanted to know. A man and woman have been shot as they were walking toward the parking lot in the mall."

"Glad you called. Rope off the scene; prevent anyone in the area from leaving. Call the medics, but don't remove the bodies 'til I get there. Should take me about twenty minutes."

Once the call with Pat ended, Zuma turned to his wife.

"Sorry, honey, yes—it's the same people we saw on TV who were introduced by the head of the Stillwell Corporation. This is going to be a mess; an interracial couple was shot. The media are going to go nuts. I can already hear the cries of racism and sexism. The pickets are going to be in front of the station by tomorrow morning."

"Joe, you've handled things like this before. You are good with the press. Just do what you do best. Find the bastard or bastards who did this. You can wake me when you get back and let me know what's going on."

Zuma kissed Claudia on the cheek, got dressed, and left. It took him twenty minutes to drive from his home, and when he arrived at the scene, he saw that Pat Vasquez had already taken charge.

"What do we have, Pat?"

"A white female and an Indian male shot in the back, close to the parking lot entrance. Several slugs in each body and a few bullet holes in parking structure. Done with a Glock 38. Not exactly a sharp shooter. No indication of a struggle or a robbery. Male is dead; female is breathing, and medics on the way. She could not speak. Purses untouched, waiting for you to make the ID official, even though I recognize them from that TV promo for Stillwell."

Zuma was careful when opening the purse of the woman and the wallet of the man so as to not smudge any fingerprints.

"Okay, Pat. It's official. We can't make an announcement 'til we notify Mr. Kumar's next of kin. Call in some other officers and have them interview everyone we have roped off to see if they saw anything about the person or persons who shot them. Have them get the names and number of anyone who has the slightest piece of information, and tell them to have the reports on my desk first thing in the morning. Let's clear the area so the coroner can get in and take Mr. Kumar down to the morgue to determine the cause of death. Make sure you tell him to put this at the top of his list. I'll call Stillwell and tell them I need the phone numbers that the two gave the company in case of emergency. I'm sure a company of that size has a 24-hour call line. I'll call Ms. Winter's family as soon as you get that number to me to let them know which hospital their daughter is in. I'll call the Kumar family as soon as I hear from the coroner in the morning so I can tell them the exact cause of death. You and I know the press will be at the precinct no matter how early we arrive. Have the hospital call us as soon as Ms. Winter is able to talk with us."

Pat admired the way Zuma went through the large number of details, all of which needed to be attended to in order to prevent lawsuits and to ensure the possible solution to the crime. He could have also done it, but he liked watching and listening to the comfortable take-charge manner that his boss had.

When Zuma got home, he found Claudia sleeping; she did not stir as he crawled into bed. He did not have the heart to wake her, and he knew that tomorrow was going to be a long day. He felt lucky and blessed to have Claudia who brought passion to her love for him and whose work as a painter of landscapes contrasted so sharply with his daily life of dealing with murderers.

His first wife, Carole, had been killed by a hit-and-run driver. The last thing he looked at before he left to work every morning was the landscape of the beach and bay in Truro, Massachusetts, where he had first met Claudia. He decided to look at it again.

He kissed Claudia gently on the cheek and pulled the covers up and over his shoulders. It took him a little longer to fall asleep than his usual two minutes as he imagined the questions that would be asked tomorrow as well as his responses.

3

Pat knew that Zuma was in a contemplative mood as he entered the precinct. One of the toothpicks, which he always carried with him, was out of his shirt pocket and in his mouth; he was humming. Pat Vasquez admired his boss's memory of songs and movies, and his ability to recall their narratives. In addition to being mentored about detective work, he was also learning about movies and music, and could often repeat lyrics that Zuma sang. He admired and respected the ability that Zuma had to relate these everyday real-life situations of crime to artistic creations.

Pat liked that he can recognize the tune and began to sing the words as Zuma hummed. "There's a calm before the storm. / Its been comin' for some time."

"You got it, Pat. I think the calm was when Fleishman was introducing his plans for Stillwell and the good it was going to bring. The rain has come and the storm is on the horizon. Ther's another song by Garth Brooks that resonates with these words but is harder to hum since it doesn't have a melody. It's called "The Thunder Rolls," and it's a great story. He's a country-estern type."

"I don't know the singer or the song, boss. Probably because I'm not a fan of country-western. Hard for me to like those moanin', sad laments. I'm much more into my Latin pop and upbeat music. You have been able to extend my tastes far beyond that but not as far as country."

"Enough with Musical Education 101. Let's get down to work. Pat, go to the board and list potential shooters of the two vics.

Hopefully, we'll hear if Ms. Water is ready to speak with us this morning. As soon as we hear from the coroner's office about Mr. Ramesh Kumar, I'm going to ask you to visit his family and inform them of their loss."

Pat went to the drawing board and began putting down names.

"What do you think, boss? Every one at the Stillwell Corp. in the artificial intelligence unit as well as Fleishman? Not sure if there was a motive for gain but could have been jealousy. They had four folks already there. So we can add the three new ones."

"That's a start. We also need to get the names of anyone the new hires were dating and any rommmates they might have had."

"I'll put someone to check the use of a Glock 38 in the past six months—either for a robbery, a shooting, or both."

"Good, Pat. Also, put out something to all our staff if they have been called in for anything involving an interracial conflict on the streets or between neighbors. Have someone check the local newspapers for the past six months to see if some interracial incident occurred where we were not involved."

Pat was taking note of his boss's orders when a woman approached them, greeting the two.

"Captain Zuma, you have two calls: One from the coroner's office and the other from San Monica hospital."

"Thank you, Heather. Pat, let me take these and if the corner confirms the cause of death, you go to the parents and I'll go to the hospital. We can meet back here for lunch at one. Here's the address for the Kumars. Do you want anyone to go with you?"

"No, boss, I think I can handle this on my own."

Joe Zuma found Sara Winter propped up in bed. Her eyes were half-closed, and she looked confused. The nurse-in-charge said that Zuma should not spend more than ten minutes as the patient was after losing lots of blood.

"Good morning, Ms. Winter. I'm Detective Joe Zuma from the Santa Monica Police Department, and we are investigating your shooting. I know this is not a great time for you to talk, but the longer we wait the more likely you are to forget matters. Can you please tell us whatever you remember?"

Zuma decided not to mention the killing of her partner to see if she had any knowledge of the shooting of her colleague.

"Ramesh and I had finished a sushi dinner on the mall, and we were walking down the parking lot. He always accompanies me to my car. The last thing I remember was hearing loud bangs and pain in my back. The next thing I knew was waking up here this morning. Where is Ramesh? Is he okay?"

Zuma paused. "Ms. Winter you and your colleague were both shot in the back. I'm very sorry to inform you that he did not survive."

Sara Winter let out a shriek and began sobbing. This continued for a few minutes; in between sobs, Zuma heard her say, "He was my best friend in grad school; we were so excited to be working together again. We were out to celebrate our continued friendship."

The nurse entered and forcefully asked Zuma to leave as the crying was not good for the patient.

"Sure, just one more question. Sara, do you have knowledge or belief of anyone who would have wanted to hurt you or Ramesh? Anyone who might be jealous of your success? Anyone who would not like to see or have a white woman and an Indian male to be close?"

"No, Detective. All of us in the artificial intelligence unit at Caltech were close and supportive; and when they found out we were leaving, they gave us a party."

"Thank you, Sara, I notified your parents before I came here, and they will probably be arriving shortly. I told them you were in stable condition."

On the way back to the precinct, Zuma got a call from Pat.

"That was a tough one, boss. Ramesh was their only child. They had sacrificed so much to support him. They left India in a thriving import/export business. The wanted him to complete his education in India, knowing that the Indian government would support gifted young people and pay for higher education. Ramesh felt the better opportunity for him was here. They did not want him to be alone in this new country and followed him here after selling their business. They asked for his body to be given to them as they would like to have him buried in India. I assumed that was fine with you, and I asked the coroner's office to help them with the details."

"Good work, Pat. No suspects there and I got nothing from my interview with Sara Winter. Let's divvy up the colleagues at Stillwell. We have Cummings, Castro, and Blackwell."

"Boss, let's—you and I—do the three of them together. We're not in a rush; we're waiting on interviews from roommates and neighbors, reports from the newspapers, and follow-up to the Glock 38."

"Good suggestion. Always good to have more ears and eyes on case, especially if they're good ones."

The toothpick was out, and Zuma was humming. Pat did not find it necessary to sing. He knew the song and knew that Zuma hummed that song whenever he was getting ready to dig deeper into a crime. The words in Pat's head were the words from the Dylan song, "The answer, my friend, is blowing in the wind / The answer is blowing in the wind."

The words gave Pat a feeling of confidence that he and his boss would find the answer to who was involved in the shooting of these two young hardworking, talented citizens. Pat had a sense of his own greater motivation because the shooting was interracial. He had experienced a lot of name-calling and hatred because he was Mexican. His father was called lazy even though he had two jobs. His mother was always thought of as an illegal while working in a market, selling food items to gringas who wanted to experiment with authentic Mexican cuisine. She knew the food they sold was not like anything she had grown up with but would not dare challenge their beliefs.

4

"Their demeanors were all different, Pat, but I think the three new hires have pretty good alibis as to where they were at the time of the shooting. We'll have to check on Blackwell and see whether he was at his mother's at Orange county for dinner. Tell her you already spoke to her son and that you got her number from him. Let her also know this is a routine investigation and she has nothing to worry about. Tell her that Jerome raved about her cooking. That should disarm her. Then ask about the times he arrived and left. Make the call now before he gets to her. Ask her what she served, and we can always ask him later if we have to. The fact that the other two were out together gives them a good alibi if they were covering something up. But the idea that they were celebrating makes sense. Let's check the restaurants to see what time they checked in for dinner and what time they left."

"Boss, none of the three hires seem like likely suspects. I don't see what the motivation would be except for—possibly—money. But none of them seemed to have money as the motivator. They loved their work and loved working together. They were tight buddies. Their styles, Blackwell's confidence, Cummings's directness and Castro's shyness made me feel they were natural and had nothing to hide. Boss, you always said the great motivators were either money, sex, or power. A modern motivator is drugs. I don't see any of those operating with these three."

"I agree. Let's see what our guys found out from the neighbors. They're usually a good source of information. The reports should be on my desk."

The officer who did the interview with James Blackwell's neighbors described how hard it was to find anyone who knew him. They knew someone had moved in recently from the furniture being delivered, but the few who saw him said he left very early and came home late. When he passed someone, he was always friendly and smiled. He never went out of his way to introduce himself. The few who had passed him recognized him from the announcement they had seen on TV when the Stillwell Corporation and the mayor were introducing the newcomers.

"Pat, the guy sounds like a workaholic. No girlfriend, works late, gets up early. I always think some workaholics have something they are hiding from or running away from. I should know. Let's keep our eyes open. It may not even be related to the shooting. What do you see in the other report, Pat?"

Cummings' neighbors described her as direct. and friendly; she knew their names but never inquired or asked questions about their lives. When she had been asked what she did, she said she worked in tech. Two of them said they were sure she was at the Stillwell Corporation because of the TV announcement, but she never said announced it to them. She had a boyfriend, but they were not sure if the guy stayed over. When neighbors passed, she introduced him as Jack. They said he seemed to avoid looking at them while she was doing the intro. I guess we need to follow up with Ms. Cummings and find out who the lover boy is."

"Yes, Pat, that sound like she is also hiding something. But again, it may or may not be related to the shootings. What do we have on Mr. Castro?"

"Our young talented Latino's neighbors said he was very friendly. He was visited frequently by who seemed to be his parents. When they left, he distributed tamales to neighbors. There was always Mexican music playing and a pretty woman who came around, but always after the parents left. She was white and no one knew her name since Castro never introduced her to anyone. They always seemed to be heading out in time for dinner. They came home early, and the music usually stopped around ten."

"Another person hiding something, but this could simply be the Latino being fearful of letting Mama and Papa knew he is seeing a gringa. You would know something about that, Pat."

"Boss, let's keep focused on suspects. That stuff happened a while back, and it's no longer true."

"So, what about Winter? She was shot; her best friend was murdered. What did her neighbors say?"

"Most of the neighbors spoke about how outgoing she was. Once she met a neighbor, she would remember their name and greet them. They knew where she worked because she had started bringing cookies home from the company that would have thrown them out. It was a nightly routine, and all the kids loved her. She only gave them to kids whose parents said it was okay to feed them. She had a regular guy friend whom she had introduced and who seemed to be her steady beau. He slept over. His name was Alex, and he is Black."

"Seems pretty strange that she did not mention him in the hospital, or she did not ask us to call him. Let's check to see if she has had any visitors besides her parents."

"Boss, there's another point in the Winter interview. One of the neighbors really disliked her and made comments about how white women were making it hard for white men because they were falling for Black guys. He was pretty awful in describing Winter. He had no shame in calling her names. The other neighbors said they knew very little about him."

"I wonder if he ever said anything to Winter and whether she was also hiding that from us."

"Boss, we got a bunch of folks who seem to hide a lot."

"Yes, we do, Pat. They had their turn to hide and now it's our turn to seek. Let's go back to Winter and find out what was going on with her and this "Make America White Again" neighbor. After we speak to her, we can interview him."

"Boss, would you explain to me about how you know something about workaholics as people who try to hide something?"

"Sure, Pat. I'll be happy to but would like to save that for a better time. How about an early breakfast tomorrow right before work?"

"That works for me."

Pat knew that Zuma would hold nothing back, and he looked forward to learning more about the man he admires.

5

"Pat, I was very much in love with my first wife—Carole. She was killed by a hit-and-run driver. I was unable to accept that our own police were never able to find the driver. I was paralyzed by this state of affairs, and I did this crazy thing. I started to track down all drivers in Los Angeles who had received a DUI charge over the past three years and made them account for their whereabouts on the night she was killed. It was also during this time that my heavy drinking began. I really thought I would kill the person if I found them. I didn't care what it might have done to my own children to have their father known as a murderer.

After a number of drivers complained to the precinct that I had harassed them about their driving record, I was asked to take a leave of absence or go on sick leave for three months. I realized that my career was in jeopardy and decided to begin AA meetings.

The meetings helped me become aware that a lot of hit-and-run drivers would not have a record. I was shocked to realize how naïve and stupid I had been. I went to meetings for ten years, and now I no longer attend as I feel in control of my drinking. The workaholic stuff was my day-and-night effort to find the person who killed Carole. What I was unable to face were my feelings of loss and helplessness. I could not deal with the fact that I was not in control of everything.

I am at peace with that feeling now. I can differentiate that which I can control and that which I can't. I had a choice to make, and I made it. Life was to go on, and I met Claudia. I discovered that it really is possible to love more than one person in a lifetime.

So that's my story, Mr. Vasquez."

Pat found the story to be very compelling. The realization that his boss had overcome such strong feeling of loss reminds him of his parents who had also overcome the daily aggressions and racial slurs they faced, as well as the loss of their country and culture.

6

Zuma and Pat found Sara Winter moving slowly down the hall, using a walker with a nurse by her side. They nodded at her, indicating that they would wait in her room.

"Glad do see you up and about, Sara. When do you think you'll be able to go home?"

"The docs say two more days maximum."

"That's good news. We thought of a few more questions we'd like to ask you. Are you up for that?"

"Sure, detectives. Any progress on the investigation regarding shootings?"

"Nothing definite as yet. We wanted to ask you about your neighbor— Mr. William Holt. He seems to be a person who has a rather intense dislike of people of color. Did he ever speak to you directly about his feelings?"

"He did, and it irritated me but because I knew how strongly he felt, I just never engaged him. He reminded me of kids on the playground who bully people but really are insecure and frightened. I felt it would be a waste of my energy. I learned that from my mother. You never let them know your feelings. If they see pain or hurt, that will only encourage them to continue."

"But you said your closest friend was Ramash Kumar. Did he ever see the two of you together? Did he say anything then?"

"Detective, if he had I assure you I would have spoken up. Ramash and I saw the glares, and after we passed him, we just laughed. We had a phrase—*another B*."

"The B standing for …?"

"Any number of possibilities, detectives. I'm sure your imaginations will not fail you."

"Ms. Winter, your neighbors told us that you have a steady boyfriend—at least they said he seemed like you're steady—and we know that he was African American. Did you have trouble with Mr. Holt about that? There must have been times when you were holding hands or embracing in public?"

"Detectives, as I said, this guy is a bully. Ramash was five foot eight and thin. My boyfriend, Robert, is six foot four and weighs 210 pounds. Holt would have been afraid to say anything. He was the typical bully, afraid to pick on someone who would not take it and probably beat the shit of him. He never even glared. He would just drop his head down whenever we passed each other."

"Thank you, Sara, and continued luck with your recovery. Here's a card. If you think Mr. Holt is doing anything to you or to others that is breaking the law, please call us. We think it is wise that you don't engage him."

Once the detectives announced their presence to William Holt, he refused to engage with them and did not let them enter his apartment.

"I see no reason to talk with you or answer your questions. Unless I am being charged, I am going to ask you to leave. If you do not, I will call my lawyer. You have no warrant. I don't want any goddam brown-skinned person in my apartment. It's bad enough that I have to see them on TV and worse that they walk on my street."

"Pat, I'm really sorry that you had to hear all that crap."

"Not to worry, boss—just another B."

"Pat, I don't think we can get a warrant to go into the guy's apartment, but we can follow him. I would guess he's probably involved in a few hate groups. Let's keep someone in front twenty-four seven so we know where he goes, who he talks to, and who visits him."

"Sure, boss, it will be my pleasure. I'll call him right now. We'll find out who the other players are on his B team."

7

"Mr. Castro, thank you for seeing us."

"You are quite welcome. This is my girlfriend, Kira Berman. Kira, I'm sure these gentlemen are here to talk about the shootings. Can she stay, detectives?"

"Of course. Do you have any suspicions about who would want to shoot Vicki Cummings and Ramash Kumar?"

"I honestly don't, detective. I have thought about it. We were all very tight in grad school and continue to be that way. We were happy to get this new position and be able to work together."

"Can you tell us where you were during the evening of the shooting.?"

Joseph Castro hesitated, and both Zuma and Pat saw it.

"It's alright, Joseph. You can tell them—No, wait, I will."

Zuma and Pat immediately recognized who was in charge of this relationship.

"Detectives, Joseph and I spent the evening here after work. We ordered dinner in. I can show you the receipt. I signed for the pizza as I was treating. We thought we might take a walk afterwards, and I'm glad we didn't. We probably would have walked on the vey mall where Joe's colleagues were shot."

"Mr. Castro, have the others who you are tight with met Kira?"

"No, they haven't."

"Can you help me understand why, since you say that you were all so tight?"

"I'm a private person, and I wanted to." Kira interrupts.

"The truth is, detectives that my boyfriend is embarrassed to be with me—his gringa. His mother comes here every week and brings him food. Before she gets here, he cleans up the places and hides my stuff. He thinks she doesn't know about me, but I think she suspects because she has stopped trying to fix him up with the daughters of the ladies she goes to church with. Joseph, I'm really tired of this cat-and-mouse game. I'm actually relieved to be able to tell someone. I need you to promise me that you are going to let her know. If you're really serious about us, you need to let her know."

"Kira, let's discuss this when the officers leave."

"I'm sorry to have contributed to your squabble; we will leave, but I have one more question. Mr. Castro, do you know where your mother was on the night that the shootings took place?"

Joseph Castro dropped his jaw and was silent for thirty seconds.

"Surely, detective, you don't think my mother…"

"It's a routine question, Mr. Castro. We need to know about the whereabouts of any and all parties who are directly and indirectly connected to the crime."

"I really don't know. She called me the morning after the shooting when she saw the news on TV, but I never asked her where she was or what she was doing when the shootings occurred."

"Thank you, Ms. Berman and Mr. Castro, for your help. If anything comes to mind, please give us a call. Good luck to the both of you."

"Wow, boss, that last one surprised me. Do you think the mom could be involved?"

"I'm not at all sure, Pat. It was a long shot. I had nothing to lose, and I thought the question could also push their relationship a bit. You know me—I'm a big one for romance."

"They seem unlikely as perps, but they did have a window of time that no one can vouch for the. Let's not rule them out."

A call came in on Pat's phone. It was the detective calling from Holt's place.

"Detective Vasquez, I wanted to keep you posted. It only took me a few minutes to get to the Holt place, and just as I got there, two guys pulled in on motorcycles, fancy rigs. Both of them were heavily tattooed. They got in the apartment quickly; they may have even had a key. After about ten minutes, the three of them came down with three cartons, and it looks like they are all leaving in one car. Holt's driving."

"Great work, Prentiss. Get the plates on the bikes and the car. Make sure you don't approach them directly. They could be armed and dangerous. Keep me posted. If they enter a building, call for a backup. They are used to being tailed, and they may want a showdown. Try avoiding shootings of any kind. Back away if they ask you to leave. They love headlines, and we don't need headlines about vigilante police officers."

"Boss, it looks like the B team has called in their A squad."

When they finally located Jerome Blackwell, he invited them to visit him at work. He informed them that at the evening of the shooting, he was dining with his mother in Orange county in Fullerton. He said he usually does this about once a month. Sometimes, they go out to dine but, on that night, they were eating at home. He left about five o'clock, stayed 'till seven, and came back to the office. A security tape would verify his coming and going that evening.

"Can you give us her number, Mr. Blackwell, so we can verify your whereabouts? Can you recall what your mom cooked for you? These are routine questions and you are not under suspicion at this time."

Blackwell gave a hearty laugh. "Detective, thank you for your assurance. Unfortunately—and don't take this personally—

assurances for Black men are always viewed as rather hollow. Here's her number. She cooked yams and made a chicken pot pie. They were delicious."

"Mr. Blackwell, can you tell Pat and I about some of the things your unit was developing?"

"I don't see how that could have any bearing on the case. This is highly secretive work. Very few people outside our unit beside Fleishman know what we are working on. Why should I tell you, detective?"

"You don't have to let us know. I'm not even sure it bears on the case, but it might. It's up to you. It could be helpful. I know that new technologies affect our police work. With this new driverless car, what do we do when there is an accident? It could be the car, but suppose the driver is loaded on something. Are they responsible? Do we have the right to evaluate the person? These are discussion that are already taking place."

Blackwell paused and thought for a moment. He decided to reveal his team's efforts, not believing that it would help lead to solving the shootings but trusting that Zuma might be able to find and do something useful with the knowledge.

"We are developing a system so that we can talk to whales and then other large species of fish. The government wants to keep them from interfering with underground warning systems. We are close to imitating their warning calls. Once we perfect these, we can install them. We are probably going to do this with other species. Warning fish that the waters are too warm or where to direct them so they can better find food would help our food supply."

"Wow. That is remarkable."

"Anything else that you want to tell us about?"

"This next one is tougher. The ocean is filled with crap, and there is a very large floating island of debris. It's called the Great Pacific Garbage Patch. It's the largest accumulation of ocean plastic in the world and is located between Hawaii and California. It weighs at least 87,000 tons. In addition to discarded plastic, it also has plastic lighters, toothbrushes, water bottles, pens, baby bottles, and cellphones. It covers an area bigger than the state of Texas. We're trying to figure out how to dissolve it without poisoning the ocean."

"Mr. Blackwell, that sounds like one wonderful project. We get to see our share of plastic right here in Santa Monica. I walk there early in the morning and I see the crap that has been washed up. The tides wash a lot of crap up, and I have seen everything you said is in that garbage patch except for cellphones. I wish you success with that one. I have an idea unrelated to this project that I just thought might help crime-fighting or crime prevention."

Blackwell laughed. "Sure, Detective, be my guest."

"People who live in a house leave a footprint of noise. The noises might vary with each person depending on their shoes or clothing, but if you could get people to record their impact of their different noises and set it up so that any strange or different noises in the house set off an alarm, it would warn the residents—it might even be set up to alert police. It's little bit like warning the whales."

Blackwell nodded his head in as if to say, 'what a good idea.'

"That's really a good one, Detective. I will have to give you financial credit if we ever can get around to developing it. Thank you."

"If there ever is a financial arrangement, I would not want it to be a personal one for me, but would rather it go to the families of police officers who have been murdered, or if I get wounded, it would help pay for my bills. I think that is probably in the future, if at all."

"Thank you, Mr. Blackwell, We will be checking with your mom and waiting for the security tape."

"Pat, let's check to see what time Blackwell came back to work. We don't have to wait for the tape. There should be a sign in sheet. Maybe a guard can confirm seeing him as well."

"Pat, let's go back to the office and put together what we got."

"What about that workaholic stuff, boss?"

"Pat, you know a hit-and-run driver killed his first wife, Carole. I was unable to accept that the police were never able to find the driver. I started to track down all drivers in Los Angeles who had received a DUI charge over the past three years and made them account for their whereabouts on the night she was killed. It was also during this time my heavy drinking began. After a number of drivers complained to the precinct that I had harassed them about their driving record, I was asked to take a leave of absence or go on sick leave for three months. I realized that my career was in jeopardy and begin going to AA meetings. The meetings helped me be aware that a lot of hit-and-run drivers would not have a record. I was buried in my work hiding from reality. The reality was that my wife had died. My plunging myself into work preventing from feeling that loss. I was shocked to realize how naive he had been. Pat, that feels like a long time ago. You know that I am in control of my drinking, and I have balance in my life with Claudia and my kids. I am blessed that that's already in the past."

The call came in as they were walking into the precinct.

"All they did was smile and wave at you and indicate they were empty-handed? No boxes? Did you follow them? Okay, so they went back and dropped Holt off, and then where did they go? You didn't follow them? Not a good move, Prentis. We've a lookout in front of the Holt place now. Go back and keep us posted on who else enters the place. Get plates and pictures of every vehicle. That shouldn't be too hard. They know they're under surveillance, and they're not afraid."

"Okay, here's what we got. Sara Water and her boyfriend; Robert Joseph Castro, his girlfriend Kira, and his mother; Vicki Cummings and her boyfriend Jack; Jerome Blackwell and his mother; William Holt and assorted bikers. I count ten. We can't exclude Fleishman and any of the other board members. So that's six or more, making sixteen."

"That's a hell of lot of work, boss."

"Right, it is. Look at the board, Pat, and think who has the most to gain? What do your instinct tell you? Who are you most curious about?"

"To be frank, boss, I'm curious as to how Kira and Castro are going to work things out. Latino and gringa stories always interest me. But that is not what you're asking me to do. The name that sticks out to me is Jack. There is a Jack on the Stillwell board and a Jack that is with Vickie Cummings."

"It's always good to start with curiosity, Pat."

"Let's go back to Ms. Cummings before we go to the board member. I'll check his name on our way over in case Vicki indicates who he is."

9

"Hi, detectives. I had a pretty good idea that you would be returning, and I can even guess what you would like to know. It's about Jack, right?"

"Yes, Ms. Cummings. Please tell us what you can or are willing to. Anything you say might be helpful to us."

"I can be open with you provided you are going to act like two clams. I have no fear of talking with you about him as I know he would never be involved with shooting anyone, but I need you to assure me that you will be discreet. I will let him know that I talked to you. I'm sure he would also want to know if what I share with you stays with the two of you."

"We will not reveal anything about your personal relationship, Ms. Cummings, but if there is anything in your story that makes us feel there is a connection to the shooting, we will follow up on that."

"Jack and I met at a conference when I was a first-year grad student at Caltech. I had delivered a paper, and he sought me out, wanting to talk about it. I'm pretty good at smelling if any male is interested in pursuing me, but I detected nothing of that nature. I believed him to be interested at only a professional level. He had perfectly good reasons to come to Caltech. He explores the artificial intelligence grad programs in the area, and he would come out to my school once or twice a year. At the end of my second year, when we were having coffee, he asked me if I was interested in pursuing our relationship at a personal level. I was surprised at the question but even more surprised at how quickly I said yes to his proposal. I was young; he was older and established at a big important company. From the beginning, we both recognized we had to keep our relationship private. If I were to get a job at Stillwell, it could never be interpreted as one I got because I knew someone, let alone be sleeping with that person. It had to be because I deserved it. Fortunately, I was brought in as part of a team so there was no investigation of who I knew. It was not too difficult to keep our relationship under wraps. My tight buddies also had coffee with Jack, so it did not seem abnormal that we had coffee more often. He was careful about hiding his interest in me to his colleagues. In fact, he told me how he mentioned to Stillwell that he would look for students at MIT and Harvard rather than Caltech."

"How did the two of you manage to keep your relationship so secretive?"

"He kept his regular apartment but found another one for the two of us. No one in his building would think it strange that he would be gone for a few days. My buddies at Caltech knew that I was close to my mom and never became suspicious if I were to also be gone for a few days. When James brought us on board at Stillwell, we were unsure as to how we were going to handle that. It's hard to hide when you're working in the same company. Besides, I was no longer a student but an employee, and intimacy is discouraged between colleagues in the same company. That's where things are as of today. I'm not sure that the shooting has any impact on us, except that it has made him more nervous. He's worried about why this new team would be a target?"

"Have either of you expressed any ideas as to why?"

"We thought about the money angle. James would have to bring in someone to replace any of us, but he would be fair and give them the same amount of money. James would reject any effort by Fleishman to reduce the salary of any incoming person, so we both rejected that possibility?"

"Anything else?"

"There's racism. Nothing overt—Fleishman is not exactly a politically correct kind of guy, but he would be shooting himself in the foot if he lost a valuable member of the Blackwell team. It would also be bad publicity for his company if an employee was shot. The only other thing is sexism."

"How so?"

"Well, you have a bunch of young kids brought in, and they are making a lot of money. Two of us are women. Some of the men and even some of the women felt they were being short-charged in salary and their loyalty to the Stillwell Corporation. They would not even have to be in the artificial intelligence unit."

"A couple more question, Ms. Cummings. Can you verify for where you were on the evening the shooting occurred? And do you own a gun, and if so, what kind is it?"

"I own a gun. It is registered. It's a Glock 38. Jack and I ordered in pizza, and he left to go back to work at around nine. I stayed in for the rest of the evening."

"Thank you, Ms. Cummings. Your personal story will stay with us and not be shared with anyone. We are going to interview Jack Knox about the theories you have proposed."

"You're welcome, detectives. I'm going to call Jack right after you leave and tell him I spoke with you and shared our personal history and that you've guaranteed discreetness."

"What do you think, Pat?"

"She sure seems mature and grounded. She was not some starry-eyed kid who was swept off of her feet by money or status. It takes a lot for a kid who is not naïve to want to be with an older established guy."

On the way to visit the Stillwell Corporation. Zuma's toothpick came out, and he began humming.

"That's a new one, boss. Never heard you do it before."

"It's a song with only two lines and has basically only twelve words. I know both the Ray Charles and Aretha Franklin version. It doesn't apply to this situation at all."

"What are those twelve words, boss?"

"Hit the road, Jack, and don't you come back / No more, no more, no more, no more / Hit the road Jack, and don't you come back no more."

"That doesn't apply at all, boss."

"I know, Pat. Some things, sometimes, just don't make sense. Sometimes, though, they make sense much later on."

10

"Detectives, Vicki called and told me to expect you. She also said she told you about our relationship. I'm happy to talk with you and help in any way I can."

"Thank you, Mr. Knox. Why don't you start with how the two of you met and how your relationship developed?"

Jack Knox recites a version of their relationship that matches the story that Vicki has related, including their debating about what to reveal to the Stillwell Corporation.

"Anything else that we need to know?"

"I've had lots of opportunities to mess around, detectives. I go to lots of schools and meet female deans, secretaries, and faculty. I have fooled around but it was different with Vicki."

"Thank you for that background, Mr. Knox. Can you tell us who you think might want two of your employees murdered?"

"I know Viki told you about our theories, so I'm only guessing about a theory of jealousy or frustration. I've looked over the promotions, and there are a few in our company who have not moved forward. We do not promote our employees automatically but promote based only on their performance. There are two people in the artificial intelligence section and two from the companies' managerial level."

"Please give us their names. We'd also like to get your permission to interview them here at Stillwell."

"I'm sure there won't be a problem with that, but I will have to let Fleishman know what you're doing."

"A couple of more questions, Mr. Knox. Do you own a weapon?"

"I do own a weapon."

"What kind?"

"It's a Glock 38. It's registered."

"I see. Can you account for your whereabouts on the evening of the shooting?"

"I left Vicki's after we had some pizza. I think I arrived here close to nine. You can check with security."

"And who else knows about your plans for these inventions you work on?"

"As I said, I think besides Fleishman there's no one else. We keep recordings of our discussions locked up. Fleishman and all members of the team have keys as they often have to go back to check something that was said."

"Boss, that list of possible suspects is growing. I think we have to regroup and go back and give some priority so we can start narrowing down suspects."

"I agree, Pat. Let's—Claudia, you, and I—go out to dinner after we do that."

At dinner with Claudia and Pat, Joe received a phone call from his older son, Josh, who informed him that he had applied for a job at the Stillwell corporation and for graduate work in chemical engineering. He had majored in biology with a minor in chemistry at UC Davis, and Stillwell was offering paid positions while supporting graduate work in exchange for three years of work after earning a PhD.

"If I get it, Dad," Josh asked, "will I be able to live with you and Claudia? I could live in the dorms but could save a lot by staying with you."

"Of course, I don't even have to check with Claudia. We have spoken about this possibility before. You will be a welcome addition to our Santa Monica home. I know some people at the Stillwell Corporation. Do you want me to make a call to see if I can help out with your application?"

"No, Dad, I want to get this on my own. Thank you for the offer."

"Okay, I will stay away from that."

"Dad, I'm not sure I'll get into UCLA, so I've also applied to UC San Diego and UC Berkeley. I'll keep you posted."

"Great. And how is your brother?"

"Dad, David is in love, and somehow, he is working harder in school than I've ever seen him do."

"It's great what love can do, son. May it happen to you soon."

"It will, Dad. I think it will happen when I'm in grad school. Say hi to Claudia for me. Love you both."

The call ended.

"I guess you both heard that possible good news."

"Yes, Joe, good news about both of your boys."

Claudia begins humming a familiar tune. Joe and Pat both break into laughter when they realized that by humming the popular Beatles song, Claudia is advising Joe to "Let It Be."

"Here's what I want to say thank you for."

Zuma hummed "Put a Little Love in Your Heart," and Pat and Claudia laughed upon hearing the song, knowing that they have put a little love in Joe's heart.

11

"We're at a dead end, boss. We don't know who shot Ramesh Omar and Sara Winter. We have no signs of the unneighborly neighbor doing anything illegal, our bikers have just been giving out leaflets, and none of the folks within the intelligence unit or the Stillwell Corporation have been linked to the shootings as they have solid alibis. It's hard to see what has been gained by anyone."

"I agree, Pat. But I don't think whoever planned this is going to stop. It's too simple a plan to have just shot an interracial couple and stop with one shooting. I think if we wait, something else will happen."

Two days later, Zuma receives the call he predicted would come. It was from Jack Knox, but it wasn't about another shooting.

"Someone broke into our intelligence unit and stole all the tapes we had. We have backup, but they are invaluable and could be sold for a very large sum of money."

"Don't touch anything, and don't let anyone—even the folks who work in the unit—enter. Stand in front of the door 'til we get there."

The careful inspection by Zuma and his team found no new fingerprints and no sign of a break-in into the safe. Someone must have used a key and had to know the combination numbers. The security guard had been knocked out with a dart that rendered him unconscious, and they had been able to disable the alarm.

"Pat, this is a very skillfully done job, done by a skillful group or an insider. It had to be more than one person since they had to get through security and stand guard while they were emptying the safe."

"I think you're right, boss, but that could include almost everyone at Stillwell or an outside team hired with information from someone inside Stillwell."

"And how far outside would the insiders have to go? I think we need to go to the FBI and Homeland Security to check to see what they have on this kind of sophisticated operation. But we also need to check phones of all Stillwell employees who made calls to numbers outside the US. We need to run lie detector tests on all employees at Stillwell, inquiring about phone calls to persons outside the US or efforts to hire anyone to do a break-in. This will be expensive, so we will ask Stillwell to pay for it. They probably will be eager to do this since they know how much their secrets could be worth if they are used. If a foreign government gets ahold of their secrets, Stillwell would be screwed."

The lie detector tests take three days to administer. Five employees refuse to cooperate. FBI and Homeland report three similar modes of operation throughout the United States but like the Stillwell theft found no pictures, no fingerprints, and no leads. The phone calls made by the five employees show that one of them had made a series of phone calls for seven days in a row. The calls had been made to the National Gun Owners publication.

A call establishing the authority of Zuma and the FBI to the National Gun Owners publication reveals that an ad had been placed by one—a Joe Zuma on a money order. The ad was short and simple, and it seemed non-inflammatory.

"Wanted: sophisticated personnel in use of undetected procedures," it states, along with a contact number.

"Boss, someone knows you and is using you. I'll call the number of that SOB. We need to bring the caller in."

"I doubt if you'll get anything, Pat. The person—or persons—must have used throwaway phones for every phone call they made."

"Mr. Fleishman, please, let's go over the security you have on these tapes. You say you have copies, so what good would they be to someone or some group?"

"No one in the US could use them because we would sue them, and all monies they made would go to us; plus, there would be damages. A foreign power or entity could use them, and we would have no way of controlling that."

"It would seem, then, Mr. Fleishman that the robbers are probably trying to sell them to a group outside the United States. Is it easy to send copies of tapes overseas? Can they be damaged in shipping or in X-raying? Is there any other way the information could be transferred?"

"It's not that difficult to protect them. But the information cannot be copied."

"That leaves only two possibilities. It's a thief—or thieves—clearly out to make money or maybe someone who just wants to create trouble for your company."

"Detective, I don't see what anyone could really gain by going to all the trouble of stealing so they could have a sense of pleasure in causing mischief. That makes no sense to me."

"Mr. Fleishman, it doesn't make sense to me either. But it doesn't have to. It just has to be a perfectly reasonable reason for the person or persons. Little boys love making mischief. Is there anyone in the company who would derive pleasure in upsetting you, and I guess I mean you personally?"

"No, Detective, I don't know anyone who would want to do that. But I don't know a lot of people who work here. Unless they report to me directly, I would not know them. I have direct contact with less than a dozen people a week. I like it that way."

"Well, we will keep pursuing the possibility of a foreign sale. If anything, or rather anyone, comes to mind who might dislike you personally and create some stress, please let Detective Vasquez or I hear from you."

The interview with Gerald Franklin proves to be unrevealing. He had called the Gun Owners Association because he wanted to buy a gun that he could use to protect himself. He kept calling to find out about its safety record and to make sure his children would not easily be able to use it in case they discovered it in his home. He indicated that the gun was now registered and available for inspection. He has not yet used it.

"Another dead end, boss. We now know the motivation. It's probably to make a buck."

"Yes, but that doesn't narrow it down. Everyone wants to make a buck. I think we need to push more on Franklin. Let's run everything we can on him. Bank statements, credit cards with new and expensive purchases, or debt payoffs."

The examination of Franklin's credit card spending and the examination of his checking and savings accounts revealed no large deposits. It was yet another dead end.

"Boss, what are we going to do with all these dead ends?"
"I don't know, Pat. I don't know."

With that, Zuma took out a toothpick and started humming.

"Okay. Boss, what's that one? I never heard it before."

"It's a Randy Newman song. Not directly related, but a couple of lines from his song about a flood in Louisiana make me feel just like this case with all its dead ends. Here are the words—'Six feet of water in / Louisiana, Louisiana / They're tryin' to wash us away / They're tryin' to wash us away.'"

"I get it, boss. All our leads get washed away."

"Pat, let's go back and review. The leads may be washed away, but we're just going have to go back into the river."

12

Josh Zuma stood at the entrance to the Stillwell Corporation and waited for the security guard to open the door.

"My, young man, you are here early. May I help you?"

"Yes, thank you. I have an appointment in HR for a job interview. It's scheduled for ten o'clock."

"You're going to have to wait a bit. Let me sign you in and give you a visitor badge so you can sit in the employee lunch room while you're waiting. I'll come and get you close to ten and take you up to HR."

The guard saw the signature and figured it was Detective Zuma's son but decided to say nothing. He thought that this is the way the world works with white people. They use their connections to help their own.

"So, what did you major in in college?"

"I was a chemistry major, but then I took an MA in engineering."

"I'm also a chemistry major, and pretty close to finishing up. Took me a long time as I had to support my two younger brothers who had special needs and my dad and mom who were too ill to work. It's been a haul, but I love chemistry."

"Me too. I love thinking about what we can do about increasing food supply and—"

"Reducing pollution. Young man, you and I are on the same page."

The next forty minutes were spent talking about chemistry—what their biggest challenges were as students and when they realized that this was what they wanted to spend their lives doing.

"Time to go, young man. Let me lead the way to your HR interview. I hope you knock their socks off."

"Thank you. I really enjoyed meeting and talking with you. Are all the folks at Stillwell as nice as you are?"

"Can't speak for all the folks, son. If you land the job, you will find out."

"Could you please tell me your name? Mine is Josh Zuma."

"Glad to meet you, Josh. I'm Ali Frazier."

Ali Frazier's mind had done a 180. He had thought this was going to be some spoiled rich kid using his parents' influence to land a job. The conversation made him realize that the kid had worked hard and really loved what he was doing. The kid was one of the few Stillwell employees who had ever asked him his name.

When Josh arrived at Joe and Claudia's home that night, he reported he felt good about the interview especially that the HR person did not ask him about a possible connection.

"Dad, I don't know if she thought it or not, but she did not ask me if I was your son. The HR person said they would get back to me in a few weeks. They needed to check my references. But the nicest time I spent at Stillwell was with an older man who was a security guard, Dad. He is studying chemistry, and he and I really hit it off. It was amazing how we both saw chemistry as being useful to deal with problems in the environment."

"Do you remember his name, Josh?"

"That's an easy one, Dad. Ali Frazier."

"With that name, he must have loved Muhammed Ali and Joe Frazier."

Zuma did not indicate to his son that the name did not register as having been part of the investigation. What did register was that a security guard had extensive knowledge and interest in chemistry.

"Claudia and I made up your bed, son. Do you need to be awakened early?"

"I do. I have an interview tomorrow at UCLA for their doctoral program, and then I have to catch the train to get to San Diego for my next interview. Wake me up at seven, please."

"Josh, I can drive you to UCLA. Joe has to be at work."

"Thank you, Claudia. That's so very nice of you. I'll say good night to both of you. I want to call David and let him know about the interview. Sleep well, and see you both in the morning."

"Joe, he is a wonderful child—no, I should say a wonderful young man. You should be very, very proud."

"I am, Claudia. I am."

13

The call came in at eleven o'clock in the morning. A standoff between police officers and some Nazi sympathizers had developed at Third Street Mall. When Zuma and Pat arrived, they saw that six officers were encircling ten sympathizers with their guns drawn. Zuma asked what had happened to get into this situation.

"They were giving out leaflets, and someone called them filthy Nazis, and one of them pulled out his gun. That's when we got a call, and we quickly came down the mall. They all had their guns drawn, and when we asked them to drop them, they asked us to get the son of a bitch who called them names. They called him a yellow-bellied liberal who didn't really believe in their constitutional right to protest. By then, the guy must have disappeared. When we asked them again to drop their weapons, they asked us to drop ours; that's where we are now."

"Thanks, Officer Singer. I'll take it from here."

Zuma had spotted Holt as one of the six and called his name out.

"I'd like to talk to you face to face. I'm handing my weapon off and am going to approach you slowly."

Zuma did not wait for a response. He dropped his holster and gun, and began slowly walking towards Holt. When he was face to face with him, he spoke.

"You got a lot of good stuff going here for your group. You were protesting as you have the right to do. Members of the press are arriving, and you'll get media attention. If you can promise me there will be no shooting, I will tell my men to drop their weapons. I can arrange for the press to take your pictures and do the interviews. Let me know now if that works. If it doesn't, I'm going to have the mall emptied. and my men will treat you and your group as hostile, refusing to follow orders and resisting arrest. You will have lost all credibility with the public, and you will be sitting ducks. I know you're smart, Mr. Holt. What do you say?"

"Men, put your guns on the ground. We will get them back later after our press conference this detective has promised we will have. I know him to be a man of his word."

The nightly news showed each of the six members asserting their right to protest their beliefs that real American heroes are neglected by the media, and too much attention is given to Martin Luther King, Jr. and Muhammad Ali. They asserted they were willing to go to jail just like Muhammad Ali.

Claudia broke into laughter when she heard them.

"Joe, they are idiots. They bemoan the attention given to Ali by the media, and they're on the media, giving him attention by identifying him as a hero for his refusal to obey the government and serve in the military."

"I know they look and sound like idiots to you, Claudia, but I think they scored some points when they accused the name-caller of being yellow bellied and refusing to debate, and when they said their views were their opinions which every American has the right to express. They seem well-coached in handling the press and ended up getting the media attention they crave and feel they need, to convince others of their views and their rights."

"Oh, Joe, I hope you're wrong."

"So do I, Claudia, so do I."

Ali Frazier watched the news conference and was amused and bitter at the kids-off- glove manner that the newscasters were responding to the pro-Nazi group. He knew that if Blacks had been protesting, and if they had drawn weapons, they would be grilled by the media. He doubted that they would have been able to leave and be booked, even if an agreement had been made. He believed that this would have been an opportunity to kill Black protestors and feed America's long-standing fear of strong Black males.

Since a few of the protestors had said that Stillwell was favoring the hiring of minorities over whites, he was sympathetic to that charge and muttered out loud but to himself: "If they only understood that it was class and not just race. Dumbbells, you get screwed—not because you're white but because you're poor and you're uneducated."

14

"Pat, let's put all possible suspects on board. If we're going to go into this river of washed away clues, we're going to have to pick up every stone again. I have an idea to list them by gender and then by race. We're working on the shootings and the theft."

"Boss, I got eight men, but we can eliminate Ramesh. We also have five women. Four of the men and three of the women are white."

"Of the men, Pat, who would have a possible motive to be involved in both crimes?"

"Only Holt and Franklin."

"Of the women, who would have a possible motive to be involved in both crimes?"

"None.

"Of the men, who would have a possible motive to be involved in only one crime?"

"Franklin."

"Of the women, who would have a possible motive to be involved in only one crime?"

"Mrs. Castro."

"Pat, so we've gone from a list of sixteen or so names to a list of three more likely suspects. We are going to monitor Franklin and Holt more carefully. If Mrs. Castro was involved in shooting Ramesh Omar and Sarah Water, she would have to know something about following them. Let's go back and ask her son, Joseph Castro, and Kirra Berman if they ever gave any information to her about where they lived. How would she have known they were going to be out that night? Let's check and see if she has a weapon. She leaves her house to visit her son on Sundays. I'd like to know about the weapon before we meet her on Sunday."

Zuma and Pat met Mrs. Edna Castro as she was pulling up to her son's house. Zuma could smell the tamales in the backseat of her car.

"We won't keep you long, Mrs. Castro. Could you tell us if you knew the address of Joseph's close colleagues at work, and if you know them, how you got them?"

"Yes, I do. I wanted to get them so I could send them congratulation and send some home-baked tamales. Joseph gave their addresses to me."

"And did you meet them?"

"No, I was supposed to, but the shooting occurred."

"One more question, Mrs. Castro—do you own a gun, and is it registered?'

"Yes, I do, and it's registered. I haven't used it for six or so months. The last time was when I was practicing on the firing range."

"Boss, I just know she is a devoted mom. She also goes to church, and I think that makes murder even less of a possibility."

"I can trust you on that, Pat. Blackwell's mom looks like she has an airtight alibi. We just ruled out the women. That leaves two men, Holt and Franklin. There's nothing we can find on Franklin. If he sold or is selling tapes, we would have found something. He is white and might have been jealous of Ramash and angry at Sarah. If he felt strongly about being passed over, his targets would not have to be race-based. Let's check and find out who which coworkers he talks to at Stillwell. We need to also check with his neighbors about what he might have mentioned to them about Stillwell."

"Looks like we are back to Holt, boss. Racism is easily a motive, and making money, as you always say, is a possibility."

"What's hard for me to imagine, Pat, is the sophistication you would need to get those tapes. It seems way beyond their abilities. I'm not saying they're dumb. Just saying that doesn't seem the way they operate. They're basically thugs. No, the tape job had to be done by someone or some group who had inside knowledge or who was quite sophisticated. We need to go though everyone at Stillwell who came close to their security operation. I'll go back to Fleishman and you go back to Knox."

15

"Dad, I'm flying back to Sacramento tonight. The interview went very well. They said they would let me know in a few days. They were sure my references would check out."

"What about your arrival?"

"No, you don't have to worry about my late arrival. David said he would pick me up. I would ask you a favor though. I want to get the phone number of that gentlemen I chatted with. His name was Ali Frazier. I don't think, if I call Stillwell, they will give the number to me, but maybe you will be able to get it. I wanted to tell him the kinds of questions they were asking me about chemistry."

"Sure, Josh, I'll try. Congratulations on the interview. Fly safe. I love you."

"I love you, Dad. And please let Claudia know what happened."

Zuma reflected again on how caring his son was about people he liked and how he would go out of his way to help in whatever ways he saw possible.

The call came in about a shoot-out.

"It's the same group that was at the mall, Detective Zuma. This time, they were on the Santa Monica pier. One of their group members was shoved and nearly fell over the rail, and when he recovered, he pulled his weapon and shot toward the crowd. We don't know if anyone was hurt. We blocked everyone from getting off the pier. The group is at the end of the pier. It's a bigger group tonight, about fifteen or so. Six of them have guns drawn while the others are at the back of the pier."

"Prentiss, they can get down the pier from the back. Get some men on the beach. And lots of them. They have to feel outnumbered and that they are all going to die if they shoot any of our guys. I'll be there in less than five minutes. You have to cover both sides of the pier."

When Zuma arrived and walked halfway up the pier, he saw that Holt was in the front line of six men with his gun drawn. Zuma asked for the bullhorn.

"Mr. Holt, I'd like to speak with you. I'll drop my gun like last time. Can you wave me to come ahead?"

Holt beckons Zuma forward.

"Good evening, Detective Zuma. I imagine you wish to make the same proposal as you made last time. That would be satisfactory to me."

"No, Mr. Holt. It's not the same proposal at all. In fact, it is not a proposal."

William Holt stiffens when hears the words, and his fist clenches around the gun.

"I'm going to give you and your men an order."

"You're not exactly in a position to give orders, detective. I have a gun; my men have guns, and your men are not likely to shoot while you are standing here."

"You're correct about all of those observations, Mr. Holt, but once again I am relying on your intelligence. If anything happens to me at your hand, can you take a moment and imagine what might happen to you, your men, and your cause?"

It did not take Holt long.

"What would you like us to do?"

"I want you to tell all your men at the back of the pier to come toward me, and call your men who are now on the beach below the pier to come up and put down their guns as you show them that you have done the same. Then I want all of your men to get down on their stomachs while we handcuff them and take them in."

"On what charges, Detective?"

"Shooting a weapon in a public area, risking the lives of citizens and threatening a police officer. There may be others that I'll figure out when we get down to the station. I have to call my men up now so they can read your guys their rights. Will you need to make one call, or will each of your guys have their own lawyer?"

"I'll make the call, detective. It will be for all my men."

The firm of Goldstein, Hovranian, and Haddad would represent the suspect and a woman named Esther Goldstein, as well as one of the other partners. Khalil Haddad showed up immediately along with three assistants after the suspects had been booked. Zuma knew Claudia would love this one. They get a Jewish, Armenian, and Muslim firm to represent them. Zuma had the idea that the money used to defend them would be coming from the national hate groups who would see it as an opportunity to get publicity.

The city district attorney argued that these men were a threat and dangerous since they had shot a weapon near a crowd and threatened a police officer. The defense team argued that only one person had shot his weapon, and there was no direct evidence that Mr. Holt had threatened Detective Zuma.

The DA indicated that the men needed to be incarcerated for at least thirty days in order to determine who had fired the weapon.

Zuma had something else in mind besides determining who fired the weapon. He saw this as a chance to solve the murder of Ramesh Omar.

16

"Pat, we need to determine the weak link in this chain of Holt followers. Someone had to be picked for the shooting. Let's figure out which one Holt would have been more likely to designate and work on him?"

Before Pat could reply, a familiar voice interrupted their conversation.

"Hi, Detective Zuma. We meet again." It was Holt. "You know, if we go to trial, it will be my word against yours. There is no evidence that I threated you. At best, it's circumstantial. I won't serve a lot of time. And we continue to get our cries out to the public of the rights of American citizens to protest. And to show our respect for Americans of every kind, we have a Jewish, a Muslim, and an Armenian firm representing us. I may serve a little time, but the publicity will be well worth it."

Zuma was unfazed. "I believe that you or one of your men, under your orders, shot and killed Ramesh Omar and wounded Sara Winter. It's only a matter of time before we can show that. The evidence will increase your time in prison quite a bit, Mr. Holt. Hate crimes are taken more seriously by courts now than they were a few years ago. If you confess now, you will serve fewer years."

"I'll take my chances, Detective." Holt took his leave.

"Pat, in looking at the information on the men who were booked along with Holt who is married or divorced but who has children."

"Two are married, and one of them has kids. One is separated and has kids."

"So if I were Holt, and I wanted to assign the shootings to someone, I'd pick the person who I would have the most leverage over. That would be anyone with kids. If they talked, they knew that Holt would go after their children. Pat, spend some time with those two."

"Boss, this is what I found out. One of the married men clearly showed indifference and anger toward his children. His kids had disobeyed his wishes too many times. The divorced man had kids who left the country with his wife—who was Mexican."

Again, Zuma marveled at the hypocrisy of these super patriots.

"Pat, let's offer whatever we can to get this one character to talk. Since you already have gotten him to talk about his children, maybe he'll be more open to your offer than to mine."

Charles Gallagher clearly loved his kids. He was only 30 years old and became attracted to Holt's group because he had been laid off from a glass manufacturing plant when Chinese workers were brought in and paid less. He was sympathetic to their cries and claims to keep Americans working and putting America first.

"Detective Vasquez, if you can guarantee that my wife and kids will be safe, I would be willing to tell you what I know about the shooting. I didn't realize that the group I was affiliated with would murder anyone. I joined them before I found out about the murder. The mall standoff showed me that they would not be eager to shoot. I was shocked about what happened at the pier. But I am afraid of Holt, his power, and his network. I'd become a target, and so would my family."

"Could you clarify something for me, Mr. Gallagher. Are you saying that when you joined the group, you knew nothing about the murder and only found out later that someone in the group had done the shooting?"

"Yes, that is what I am saying."

"We can offer to put you and your family in a witness protection program. I have to check a few things before I make a definite offer. It would be federally sponsored as this is a hate crime and the group you belong to has national interstate connections."

"Good job, Pat. Before we make an offer to Gallagher, let's figure out the guy whom Holt would believe is the strongest and has the least to lose."

"Boss, while you were talking to Holt at the mall, I kept noticing how he was looking at one of his men. It was the same one that was leading the pack in from the back of the pier. My guess is that he would be second in command. His name is Covington—Lester, Covington."

"Pat, let's pay Mr. Covington a visit and see if Lester is more rather than less involved in a murder."

The visit proved to be fruitless. Covington was not worried about any testimony that would definitely link him to the shootings. He indicated that, at best, it would be hearsay evidence. It was clear to Zuma and Pat that this guy had always been prepared to do some time in service of the cause. The witness protection program was offered to Gallagher, and he was immediately put into isolation so that nothing would happen to him while he was in prison. The detectives knew the isolation of Gallagher would alert Holt. They would have to get something on record immediately, just in case.

Holt's long arm would eliminate Gallagher from testifying what he knew.

After Gallagher agreed to the offer of witness protection, Zuma and Pat got a videographer to record the interview.

Gallagher reported that he heard Lester Covington brag about how he had shot "one brown dude and his probable white chick girlfriend." The interviewer established that those were his exact words, and they were said in front of two other men besides Gallagher.

The moment the interview was finished, Zuma turned to Pat. He spoke in quiet and what sounded like an angry tone.

"That's not going to help us one damn bit to get a conviction, Pat. We will not get any of the others to testify that they heard those words. It's one man's words against a wall of silence and coverup. We've got to go ahead with the offer to Gallagher, but we should not use this tape in court. It will definitely work against us. We need to find another way to get Covington."

17

The trial for the men in the Holt group took two weeks. The city attorneys who were on the TV every night with the progress of the trial saw it as an opportunity to show the public that these law breakers were not being charged because of protesting but because they had violated city ordinances reading public safety. The usual concerns about spending money were dropped as the feelings in the office were that this was good publicity and could be used to get more budget for next year. The defense team also saw it as an opportunity to get publicity and were in no rush to diminish the expenses of Holt's pro-Nazi group. Without knowing it, each group had its own reasons for keeping the trial going as long as possible. The attorney for the city did this by insisting that each person be called upon to testify. The defense team did this by showing that each of the men who were called upon to testify were shown to have spotless records, employed with jobs, and had no debts. Zuma was hoping that the costs, which he estimated were $15,000 a day, would become upsetting to the national groups who would now have to foot the bill for $150,000. Zuma also knew, because one of the partners had told him, that ten percent of the costs in the case would be donated to organizations working to disseminate information and fighting the hate propaganda.

The jury came back with fines of $5,000 for all the men—except Holt and Covington who were each sentenced to 30 days in jail, fined $20,00, and given two years of parole.

The day the men were released, Zuma approached Pat and proposed his plan to catch Holt and Covington.

"Pat, you're going to find four white officers who are youngish, and you will educate them in the beliefs of this group. They need to be informed that they will be going undercover to infiltrate Holt's group. Screen them first. Hopefully, you can find four without families. We don't want any of them to be concerned or frightened about repercussions to their loved ones. We will be sending in all four even though we only need two. I want Holt to discover that two of them are spies for us. We can give two of them weak cover stories. An employment number that doesn't exist or a home address that is totally off would probably work. When Holt dumps them, he will feel he's out of the woods. We should have two of our men ensconced in the group who will acknowledge being married, and we will have two female officers planted in an apartment who will identify themselves as the wives of the two men. The wives and the men will report directly to you, Pat. They will need phones that can be discarded so no traces can be made. Do not tell the two men with weak stories that we expected them to be discovered. That they did not make the cut will ensure that the ones who get through have to be aware of how cautious they have to be about hiding their identities. All the men need to be notified that this is an extremely dangerous situation. If Holt's men get suspicious, they could easily murder them and fabricate a story about a brawl that got out of hand. Pat, do we have four white young men?"

"I'm pretty sure we do, boss. I will train them, and they will be ready in time to play ball for the B or the A team."

Claudia and Joe watched the trials proceedings every night on TV. They were pleased with the dignity that the city attorney was giving to the accused and enjoyed the publicity that the defense team was getting. One reporter decided it would be a good human-interest story if Stillwell employees would talk about the impact of the trial on employees.

All of them, including Fleishman, were pleased with the proceeding and believed the men would be given a fair day in court. One employee, Ali Frazier, was also pleased but surprised that the city attorney had pursued the case so rigorously. When asked why, he replied that most of the time, when a man of color is murdered, cases would not be pursued as vigorously. He surmised that the attorney's office received pressure from the public that would not approve of an interracial couple being shot at, especially when one member of the couple was white. He mentioned that men and women of color are often ignored in public and at work.

The interviewer saw an opening.

"Mr. Frazier, are you ignored at the company you work in?"

Frazier paused. This was his chance and might be his only chance where it would not seem that he as a Black man had an ax to grind but could be delivering a message to a possibly receptive wide audience.

"You can be ignored in a number of ways, Mr. Cranston. Sometimes, people will never know your name or remember it incorrectly. Sometimes, people will pass you and not recognize you."

"And Mr. Frazier, have either of those forms of ignoring been your experience while working at Stillwell?"

"Of course, they have. I'm Black."

"Thank you, Mr. Frazier." And with that the reporter turned to the camera.

"You have just heard the experiences of a man who has worked at a company for ten years as a security guard, is studying to complete his bachelor of science in chemistry at a local university, but is a relatively unknown to his coworkers who ignore him. How many others who have seen this interview can verify their experiences at their employment sites as similar? We invite you to call in and tell us about your encounters in places of your employment. If you wish to be anonymous on your phone call, please say so. If your work life as men or women of color is different than the one you heard tonight, we will be happy to report that also. Until then, this is Allan Cranston, reporting from Santa Monica."

"Joe, isn't that the man who Josh talked about?"

"Yes, it is, Claudia. I'm going to call Josh to see if he heard the interview." Before Joe could get up from the couch, the phone rang, and it was Josh.

"Yes. I saw it, Dad. I know the guy, and he has seen a lot of crap happen to his people in our country. He may not have caught up to the idea that many white Americans now get upset when a Black or man of color is murdered or overlooked for a job, or is fired ahead of whites even though the Black man has seniority. I understand where he might be coming from. I know that even now, many white people still do not see a person of color who walks past them. I'm going to call him tonight and congratulate him on the interview. He was honest and not pulling his punches."

"Joe, I think your son Josh is ahead of us in our understanding of race relations."

"You're probably right, Claudia. I'm going to check with Pat tomorrow on what Frazier and Josh said about being ignored."

18

Two of the men that Pat had selected for infiltrating never got past the application. They were never called back, which was the plan that Zuma and Pat had developed. The two others were invited to a meeting with Holt and Covington. They were grilled about their reasons for wanting to join the group. Apparently, they passed the tests because they were invited to a meeting to be held the next night. Pat and Zuma were able to observe the officers handing out leaflets in the mall and shouting slogans about the importance of building a wall in promoting judges who were in favor of keeping the constitution and not changing it and asking for donations.

Two weeks had gone by, and the two officers told Pat that they had passed the point where their loyalty might be challenged.

"Good. I'd like the two of you to start wearing a wire. After your days or evening work for the group, I assume that a few of you go to a bar and hang out."

"Yes, we do. It's pretty much a regular thing. They like to drink and tell stories. They really drink. We have trouble keeping up with them."

"That's the advantage of a wire. You can be loaded, but the tape won't lie. You have done great so far. It's good that you are avoiding interviews at the mall from reporters. Someone might recognize you. If someone at the mall does recognize you, I want you to just walk away. I don't want you to be grilled. Just assume that the recognition, even though the person is asking a question, is enough to blow your cover. Do you get it? No *if*s, *and*s, or *but*s. I don't care how far you've gotten in. You would be in great danger. If you get something on the tape that incriminates Holt or Covington, don't do anything. Just come in the next day with the tapes. We'll take it from there. It can be either one, but try to get evidence on both of them. Our suspicion is that Holt gave the order, and Covington was the hitman."

In the bar that evening, one of the undercover officers addressed Holt directly.

"Mr. Holt, I admire the way you seem to be fearless about continuing. You've had two encounters with the goddamn cops, and you don't seem to be fazed."

"It's easy, son. I believe in the cause. I love our country, and I hate seeing where it is headed."

"Kid, he's our leader, and he always calls the shots. He is very smart. We got away with something big. Do you remember that shooting at the mall? A fucking Indian was shot as well as his white girlfriend."

"Slow down. Ease up. You're giving away top secrets."

Covington spoke, "Aw, come on. These new guys have proven themselves. They really get into it at the mall. They're clean cut compared to us, and because they're younger, I think they get through to lots of passersby. William Holt, you know how much we respect you, and I wanted to show it to these new kids."

Holt had already been impressed with the younger newbies. He imagined that they were clearly next in line to Covington. He nodded his head to Covington as if to say go ahead and talk.

"Many of us saw the new Stillwell appointments on TV. A bunch of new coloreds and women coming to live and work in Santa Monica. We were all pissed, but only Holt figured out we could use this to make our point. We knew what they looked like from TV, and we waited a few nights before we could follow them to where they lived. After that, it was just a matter of time before we could move in on them. It was our lucky day when two of them left the woman's house and went to the mall. I am a pretty good shot, but somehow, I missed the woman. Holt wasn't pissed at me for only wounding the woman. He felt the message he asked me to deliver had been sent. I told you, didn't I, William, that I'd be happy to go after the others? You told me that you would not be giving me any more orders to take anyone out. I was disappointed that I wasn't given another assignment. I was itching to show that I was a better shot."

"You got it exactly right, Lester. I never doubted that you were a bad shot when you only wounded the girl. I'd call on you again if I had to. Now, let's have a drink, toast to our newbies, and say goodnight. I need to figure out another place in Santa Monica where we can get some more publicity. We get lots of applicants when we get publicity, but we can't keep going back to the same spot. People will get used to us and just pass us by. If any of you have some ideas, please call me and just leave the name of the site."

One of the undercover agents called and left the name of the site. "Santa Monica Police Station."

It was the easiest arrest Zuma and Pat had ever made. They walked up to the line of protestors singled out Holt and Covington and told them they were being arrested and would be charged with the murder of Ramesh Omar and the shooting and attempted murder of Sara Water.

"I'll read you your rights, and then I'll give you my phone so you can call your law firm."

The judge agreed that there would be no bail as the two were flight risks and would remain in jail, until the trial.

The lawyers for Holt and Covington told them the evidence was solid. At best, if they pleaded no contest, Covington could get life sentence and Holt would get thirty years. Covington refused. He would go to trial and face the consequences. He was not afraid of dying for the cause. Holt pleaded. He got a sentence of thirty years.

19

"Boss, we got one murder solved, and one theft that is still unsolved. The Santa Monica Post Office has not traced or found anything being sent out that looks suspicious. If it was sent from some other station, we would never be able to know anything. So far—nothing."

"Pat, we may never know anything unless another foreign entity produces the technology or equipment. It will be a loss for Stillwell. Bu no one will be hurt except for the Stillwell investors."

"Boss, it seems that the theft and the murder were not related. I guess we can assume that some other person or persons were involved. Where does that leave us?"

"It leaves us with a folder that we will file under 'Unsolved Thefts.' In the meantime, I just got some very good news."

"Oh?"

"Josh has been accepted at Stillwell and at UCLA, and will be living in UCLA's graduate housing. Stillwell will be paying his tuition and living expenses for all four years of his doctoral work. All he has to do is work for their company for three years after his degree."

"That is good news, boss. It should make you and Claudia happy to be able to see him more frequently."

"Maybe, but you can never tell. Doctoral work can be very time consuming. I might have less contact now than when he was living in Davis."

Josh and his brother David drove from Sacramento in a U-Haul with the furniture that Josh would be using for housing while he was at UCLA. The two brothers, along with Pat, Claudia, and Zuma, had dinner together before David headed back. Even though he was just gone for one day, he was anxious to see his girlfriend.

It was another two weeks before Zuma heard from his son suggesting dinner.

"They are really nice to me at Stillwell. They introduced me to the entire company on FaceTime so people would recognize me and not look at me suspiciously if they saw me. Fleishman told me that I got the job before he knew I was related to Zuma. He asked me if I knew how you were able to get the respect of the Santa Monica community. I referred him back to you, Dad. Fleishman also invited me to sit on a meeting of the artificial intelligence group. That was fun and oh-so-interesting. It's the exact kind of stuff I hope I will be doing after my degree. I've also had lunch a couple of times with Mr. Frazier. He and I still love to talk chemistry. I wanted to tell him about what the intelligence unit was working on, but Fleishman said I was not allowed to talk to anyone about it."

Zuma had never seen his son so excited about his life. He was basking in the excitement and wasn't sure if he was warm from Josh's excitement or from the delicious salmon that he had just eaten.

"Do you need anything from Claudia or me, Josh?"

"No, Dad. You have been wonderful, and so has Claudia."

It was the day after dinner that Zuma got the call from Fleishman about training the Stillwell Company about matters of respect and civility. He thought of the irony of a Nazi sympathizer group being responsible for this turn of events. The people they hated will now be treated more civilly.

"I'll be glad to come in with Pat Vasquez, Mr. Stillwell. No, I can't charge a fee. You could make a donation to the Policemen's

Association. They are in dire need of money to take care of the great increase in officer shootings that have been incurred in the line of duty. Money is also given to their families for basic necessities. You don't have to do anything with your staff right now. Pat and I would want to meet with you to discuss possibilities and make recommendations. If you approve, we can go from there."

"I can't imagine anything you'd suggest that I wouldn't approve of. I met your son and if you can do even a little bit for us as you have done to and for him, I will be totally on board."

At the table that Claudia had reserved at the Shangri-La, Zuma had ordered a scotch and soda, and Josh ordered the same. Zuma was surprised at Josh's order but said nothing, realizing that there must be lots of things that Josh did now that he did not know about.

The call came in from Pat Vasquez as they were enjoying their dessert.

"Boss, Lester Covington was murdered. He was stabbed while walking in the prison yard. One of the members of the Holt gang has requested his body be returned for a local funeral."

"Pat, we're going to have to monitor the funeral. This will be an opportunity for them to marshal forces again and get publicity. We need to be prepared for the possibility that Holt will be seeking a pass to speak at this shindig. Covington has no family, and the judge may honor his request."

"I guess the Aryan Nation, even with their extensive network in and out of prisons, could not protect him from the brothers. You know, boss, I've always had this strong belief that what goes around comes around. Maybe it will also happen at Stillwell."

20

"Pat, you, Frazier and I will have a meeting this afternoon at three with Fleishman and Knox."

Fleishman started the meeting.

"Before we get started, I wanted to say I saw you on TV, Mr. Frazier, and I was impressed by your candor."

"Thank you, Mr. Fleishman. Was that the first time you have seen me?"

"Yes, I'm embarrassed to say it was."

"That's what I'm sure we need to address in this meeting. I have seen you quite often, Mr. Fleishman. A conservative estimate would be five hundred or so times in the ten years I have been here. That number is for just once a week, even though I know it's more."

There was a long silence before Fleishman spoke.

"I'm sorry. I guess it's because we never spoke."

"Ah, but we have, Mr. Fleishman. You and I had a mini conversation. It was mini because you didn't let me finish. You cut me off. You were not interested in what I was about to say."

There was another even longer silence before Fleishman spoke and said simply, "I'm very, very sorry."

Zuma waited a full minute, wanting to make sure that Fleishman had absorbed what Muhammed had said. When he saw Fleishman look up, he began.

"Okay, gentlemen, Ali has brought up some of the issues that go on at Stillwell. He has pointed out that there is a pattern at Stillwell of 'not seeing people, not knowing people, and not talking to people'.

I want us to throw list some ideas of how each of us we might change the culture at Stilwell. Here's one that Pat and I have used before: Each table in the lunch room cannot be exclusive for one level of people in the company. Every table with its eight seats must have at least three levels of employees."

Knox came up with the next one. "The 15-minute break should not be given to one level. We can mix levels because that's when people talk to each other."

Ali came up with the third one. "We have recreational teams in the company. A bowling, basketball, or baseball team—depending on people's interests. Each team must have different levels. Everyone is assigned to a team, even if they have no interest. And they must show up, or else there will be a penalty."

Fleishman spoke. "I think these are interesting and probably useful ideas. I think they will cost the company lost time in productivity and, therefore, earnings. I'm not sure I or my board will fully support them."

Zuma spoke, "These ideas and others that may develop will, in the long run, help earnings. There will be better morale, less absenteeism, less turnover with satisfied and loyal employees. You will get lots of publicity for Stillwell as the company where employees are happy. This will be good publicity for the city of Santa Monica as well. Your job, Mr. Fleishman, is to back them up with these proposals. Without your commitment, none of these will succeed. Your employees must feel that this is the Stillwell policy that the top dog believes in and wants. Stillwell is your baby, and you want to see it grow. While you're planning to speak to the board—which I assume you will do—can you, Mr. Knox, figure out a way to implement numbers one and two? We also need that survey for number three. Can you find someone who can do that?"

"It will be done. When do you want to meet again?"

"I think a week of time should do it."

Holt's lawyer sought out a Jewish judge, believing they would not want to be accused of bias and would lean over backwards to give him the privilege of speaking at a close friend's funeral. It worked. Holt was released. The funeral had about twenty attendees but the crowd of people protesting silently at the grave side was enormous. When Holt began his eulogy, their cries and chants of 'kill fascism, kill fascism' made it impossible for any of the attendees to hear Holt. When he realized this, he just stopped and walked away. The police had difficulty protecting him from the crowd, but he was safely shuffled off into the armored security van. But getting in, he turned to the chanting crowd and gave the Sieg Heil salute. Zuma knew that when the salute would be shown on TV and seen by Black inmates, the Aryan Nation would not be able to protect him for very long.

21

Zuma got the call from Fleishman coming in at nine o'clock on the day of the scheduled meeting. He assumed it was to report what the board said, but when he heard the excitement in Fleishman's voice, he knew that the call had nothing to do with the board meeting.

"The tapes are back. One of the early employees found a package at the entrance, and security called me. I told him to X-ray them and get back to me. He did, and said there were some kinds of tapes in there. I'm at the office now, and Jack and I have verified they are the same tapes and have not been tampered with."

"Pat and I will be right there. So, at this point only the security guards and your fingerprints would be on the package?"

"Yes, his and mine. I cut the package open with a scissor. They are the tapes that have been stolen."

Pat and Zuma could find no other fingerprints nor was there any postage or anything else that revealed who might have been in possession of the tapes.

"This is very good for your company, Mr. Fleishman. Do you have anything else to report that is good for your company?"

"Yes, I do. The board is on board. And I am fully on board."

"Great. Pat and I can leave the two of you to start implementing these plans. You need to communicate in multiple ways that this is the new policy at Stillwell, and you as president stand fully behind them. Use e-mails—personal and professional, phone calls, and any other forms of communication used at Stillwell. Let the employees talk about it, and converse with each other for a week before you actually implement the proposals. Check back with us after a week to see how the implementation is going. If you need any help, call us. Pat and I will help in any way we can."

"Good morning, Mr. Frazier."

"And a good morning to you, Mr. Fleishman. You seem especially exuberant today."

"I am. I got a great present. And it was a complete surprise."

"I guess great presents are like a Stork dropping a baby on your doorstep. Or maybe at your place of work."

Fleishman stared at Ali who stared back. Their eyes were locked until a glimmer of understanding appeared on Fleishman's face. The glimmer changed to a smile and a nodding of the head as if to say, 'I get it'.

That afternoon, in Ali's e-mail, there was a message from Fleishman.

"You will be given four years of fellowship support and living expenses conditional upon your agreement to work for Stillwell for three years upon completion of your doctoral work. Effective immediately is a 20 percent increase in your salary."

"Boss, what do we do with this folder? It's a theft where the goods have been returned. We can't leave it as 'Unsolved Theft'."

Zuma laughed. "I don't know, Pat. Why don't you go ahead and make up a new title?"

"This has been a weird case, boss. There was only one shooting resulting in one dead with lots of suspects, and a theft with lots of suspects. We ended up not solving the theft and getting the perpetrators who were the most suspicious suspects from the beginning. And the other weird thing, boss, is that you did not do a lot of humming. I missed that."

A call from Ali Frazier came in for Zuma. He wanted to celebrate the good news about the fellowship award and increase in salary.

"I've already told Josh that I might be a year behind him at UCLA so he should save his books for me."

The drinks, food, and service at a new Thai restaurant that had opened at the mall were excellent. Zuma and Claudia were excited to think they would be able to see Josh more often and happy that he might have a close friend at UCLA. For one of the few times in his life, Zuma could not think of a song he wanted to hum. It was Josh who began singing the Paul McCartney song "Hope for the Future," and Claudia quickly joined him. Zuma smiled deeply, feeling the torch was being passed on. He also thought that Covington's murder and Holt's probably soon-to-happen murder would supply a lot of fuel for recruiting. He knew his department would be facing a lot more hate crimes in the very near future.

www.ingramcontent.com/pod-product-compliance
Lightning Source LLC
Chambersburg PA
CBHW021451070526
44577CB00002B/351